STRE

SURVIVAL
KIT

52 Stress Management Tools

Volume I

Bob Czimbal & Maggie Zadikov

Edited by L. Tobin
Illustrated by D. Setoda

OPEN BOOK

Open for the adventure of a lifetime.

STRESS
SURVIVAL
KIT

52 Stress Management Tools

Volume I

Bob Czimbal and Maggie Zadikov

Edited by L. Tobin
Illustrations by Dodie Setoda

Dedicated to
Daniel Ransohoff

A man who is my friend,
a teacher who inspired me to learn from everything in life,
a role model of what giving is all about,
a person who has a clear vision,
a lecturer and photographer who reminds us of
the work that must be done.
With thanks. Bob Czimbal

© 1992 Czimbal and Zadikov

Open Book Publishers
2501 SE Madison, Portland, Oregon 97214

(503) 232-3522

First printing, Spring 1992   ISBN 1-878793-02-0
Second Edition, Winter 1993   ISBN 1-878793-03-9

1. Stress management. 2. Health. 3. Self-help. 4. Humor.

Notice: This book provides suggestions and information toward greater health and wellness. It is not meant as a substitute for a visit to a health care professional or counselor. Final judgement on the applicability of these suggestions toward individual concerns rests solely with the reader. The authors, editor and publishers shall have neither liability nor responsibility to any person or entity with respect to any loss or damage caused, directly or indirectly, by the information in this book.

Contents

Basic Stress Survival Course

52 Survival Tools

Resources

Introduction

Congratulations, you are a survivor! Through sometimes difficult times, you made enough good decisions to stay alive. You learned the skills you needed to arrive at this point in life safely.

Now that your life has moved beyond questions of daily survival you have the time and energy for greater growth and happiness. Beyond survival, all of life becomes an adventure.

However, all adventures require continued attention to skills that ensure health and safety. Even on a Sunday afternoon hike in the wilderness it is wise to take along a survival kit. Such emergencies as becoming lost, injured or caught in foul weather can occur. A wilderness survival kit might include compass, map, matches, tarp, flashlight, knife, first aid kit, signaling device, extra clothing, food and water. These simple, practical supplies may be crucial to protect yourself, minimize suffering and return safely home.

It is rare that anyone is lost in the wilderness these days. Everyone has times of feeling temporarily lost.

You are born with the will to live. When pushed to the edge, the skills you have learned can make the difference between falling or rappelling to safety.

The Stress Survival Kit contains essential survival tools for your journey through the years ahead. These practical stress management ideas will help you be well prepared for a crisis.

The Basic Short Course in Stress Survival and the 52 Survival Tools will help make your life challenging and exciting.

Basic Stress Survival Course

Stress or Distress

Everything you do creates a certain amount of stress: eating, working, driving a car and relationships. Everyone needs a certain amount of challenge and change to be healthy.

Daily stress is natural, necessary and unavoidable. How well you handle stress determines whether you experience an event as a helpful or harmful. The survivor's goal is to maintain a comfortable and productive level of daily stress.

When you exercise, you stress your muscles, heart, lungs and circulatory system in a healthy way. Just the right amount of exercise helps your body become stronger. Too little exercise and you get out of shape, while too much exercise will cause you pain.

Similarly, you need to maintain just the right level of stress to function best. Too much or too little stress can take you beyond a comfortable feeling toward distress. This anxious distress that you experience when overworked or bored places a tremendous strain on your body. Distress can cause health problems over time.

Distress occurs whenever your level of stress is beyond your ability to cope. When distressed, the degree of wear and tear on the body has become greater than the amount of rest and repair. Distress is uncomfortable and painful.

Stress Management

Change is always stressful and demanding. When poorly managed stress can have a negative impact on all areas of your life.

Stress management techniques teach you to confront stressful events in productive and healthy ways. Each person needs to develop a personal strategy for managing stress that works best for him or her.

Stress management is an essential part of everyone's life. The goal is to diffuse distress quickly and not to inflict your distress and pain upon others. In this way, you can avoid an explosive chain reaction of your stress colliding with the stress of other people.

Managing your stress more effectively may involve reducing stress or adding healthy challenges to your life. Your personal strategy may include learning to eliminate stressors or removing yourself from unhealthy situations. You can learn to cope more effectively and counterbalance stress by increasing recreation and support. Whatever strategy you choose will also serve as a healthy example for others in your life.

Stress management is an essential part of a wellness lifestyle. Good stress management and healthy daily activities enhance your well-being. Through a wellness lifestyle that includes daily exercise, good nutrition, relaxation techniques and stress survival skills you can learn to manage all aspects of your life more effectively. Success at managing stress will be reflected in both improved health and self-esteem.

Stress management equals life management.

Life in the Comfort Zone

When you are managing stress effectively you are living in your Comfort Zone. Your Comfort Zone is developed through healthy lifestyles, positive attitude, exercise, quality relationships and the many ways you nurture yourself.

Learning the skills of stress management helps you increase the size of your Comfort Zone. Staying in your Comfort Zone simply means you spend more time feeling great. When unexpected stresses do occur, a person centered in his or her Comfort Zone will be less likely to fall into distress.

The Stress Survival Kit gives you 52 tools in the next section to build your Comfort Zone. A large protective shield is able to deflect excess stress that might otherwise wear you down.

The list below describes how people feel when they are in their Comfort Zone. How much of your time is spent in the Comfort Zone?

affectionate	alive	alert
playful	productive	motivated
energetic	challenged	relaxed
enthusiastic	optimistic	resilient

Comfort Zone

Warning Zone

Distress Zone

The Warning Zone

Your body warns you of impending distress. Your warning indicators–physical, emotional and behavioral–can be signs of either too little stress or too much stress. Either extreme can be equally dangerous.

When a person has too little stress, then he or she experiences rust out. The lack of challenge or change in life brings feelings of boredom and despair. Life feels unexciting, uneventful and blah.

A person with too much stress experiences burn out. Feeling out of control creates aggravation and exhaustion.

Discomfort and pain are the warning signals to take appropriate action to manage your stress. Severe problems may develop if these warning signals are denied or covered over with drugs.

Listed below are typical warning indicators of distress. Stress may play a minor or major role in any of these symptoms. Learn to recognize early warning signals of stress in your own life.

Which of these common physical, emotional or behavior indicators are warning signs of distress for you? What additional warning signals of distress do you experience? Do you tend to rust out, burn out or do you experience both?

Physical	Emotional	Behavioral
muscle tension	anxiety	overeating
cold or sweaty hands	fear	drug use
headache	loneliness	sleep problems
diarrhea/constipation	helplessness	careless driving
menstrual concerns	loss of humor	forgetfulness
impotence	depression	sexual problems
fatigue/weariness	anger	loss of productivity
ulcers	irritability	confusion
skin problems	impatience	low concentration
indigestion	resentment	self-destructive behavior
nervous tics	instability	relationship troubles

Distress Zone

Distress occurs when the strain of life becomes greater than you can handle. Distress is a painful and exhausting experience.

You may find yourself abruptly thrown from your Comfort Zone directly into your Distress Zone from an unexpected avalanche of excessively stressful events. If you are living on the edge of your Warning Zone, one small additional stress may be all it takes to push you into distress.

Major sources of distress include illness, relationship difficulties and money problems. Distress may also be the result of minor daily tensions not sufficiently discharged or conflicts left unresolved. Your attitude plays an important role in the severity or length of distress. The earliest signal that you are not managing stress well may be the loss of your sense of humor.

Distress can be life threatening. When one aspect of your life is in distress there is a corresponding strain on all other parts of your life. Distress can cause soul scars, painful life experiences that damage the spirit.

The goal of stress management is to prevent distress whenever possible. When you notice you are in distress act quickly to return to your Comfort Zone. A downward spiral of distress is difficult to stop. Vast amounts of energy will be expended to reverse this momentum. It takes time to recover from distress.

The following common descriptors indicate that you are in distress. Time to take action.

dis-eased	disagreeable	disappointed
disconnected	discontented	discounted
discouraged	disgraced	disheartened
disliked	distrustful	disturbed
dismissed	disowned	displaced
disregarded	disrespected	dissatisfied

Stress Self-Evaluation

When you encounter stress or distress, it is helpful to be able to accurately describe what you are experiencing. Then you will be able to choose the most appropriate course of action.

Is my stress:

- small or large
- familiar or new
- imagined or real
- short or long term
- slow or fast paced
- single or several in a row
- enjoyable or life threatening
- accidental or lifestyle induced?

Which of these statements describe my stress management abilities and which require additional attention?

I can handle being under pressure.
I recognize when my energy is getting low.
I have ways to release tension constructively.
I take time out to calm down after a stressful event.
I know what raises and lowers my ability to cope with stress.
I give myself permission to take breaks when under extra stress.
I actively make changes in my life to keep stress at a healthy level.

My stress management goals are to:

- maximize the daily pleasures
- eliminate the stresses I do not want
- create the positive stresses I need
- create healthy releases for tension
- minimize current painful distress in my life
- feel confident in my ability to manage stress
- raise my ability to thrive during times of stress
- create a healthier daily environment in which to thrive.

Questions of Survival

Below are a number of questions that will help you to understand stress.

- Am I living the life I want?

- What attitudes cause me distress?

- When am I most vulnerable to distress?

- What are my major sources of distress?

- Is my stress level rising, falling or stable?

- What negative stresses can I remove now?

- Which positive stresses do I want to experience?

- What kind of stress do I need to learn to handle better?

- What am I willing to change at this time to accomplish my goals?

- What circumstances or events keep me on a high pitch of stress?

- How does distress affect my relationship with family, friends and coworkers?

- How much time, energy or money will I need to invest to manage this stress? Is it worth the investment?

Beyond Fight or Flight

The often mentioned
"fight or flight response"
presents two extreme reactions
to distress. In primitive times,
these options were used when
confronted with life-threatening
dangers.

Human survival relies upon our inborn, automatic response to
threats that trigger within us a series of physiological changes:
increase in heart rate, breathing and adrenaline. These involuntary
responses prepare us to meet whatever demanding circumstance you
face.

Today there are still times when to stay and fight for your rights
remains the best course of action. It is also sometimes wise to take
flight when a dangerous situation arises; for example, when you are
faced with the threat of physical harm.

There are times when neither fight or flight is appropriate. For
example, when your boss is angry, you need a wider range of choices
other than fighting or fleeing.

The real threat today is finding yourself living in a constant state
of alert. When these physical preparations are continuous, the
tension becomes exhausting to both the body and mind. Relentless
distress can seriously impair health, causing the body to wear down
faster than usual, ultimately resulting in premature death.

To demonstrate just how automatic your response system is,
imagine yourself making homemade chili. See yourself adding
onions, garlic, chili powder and jalapeno peppers. Notice that your
mouth is salivating just thinking about chili. Even though you are not
going to eat the chili, your body still prepared you to digest this spicy
meal.

If you focus on chili, you will salivate whether you want to or not.
Similarly, if you dwell on imagined problems, you can unnecessarily
elicit the distress response.

Because of the automatic response to both real and imagined
problems, it is essential to be careful about what you focus your mind
on. In the face of modern stresses, you need a wide range of
responses from which you can draw at a moment's notice.

The Survival Responses

The Survival Responses represent a variety of effective actions that will enhance your well being and help you avoid distress.

The Survival Responses are not inborn responses; they must be learned. The survivor chooses the courses of action that will best ensure survival and enhance health and happiness.

When daily struggles exceed your abilities to manage them, Survival Responses help you return to your Comfort Zone.

What will it be in your life: fight, flight or flow? Flow describes the survivor's determination not to be stuck with just two primitive reactions. The survivor creed is: "I will do whatever it takes to survive and grow stronger."

For example, when faced with distress, a survivor could practice assertiveness first rather than resort immediately to fighting. Rather than fleeing, a survivor might choose to flow with a sense of humor. A survivor chooses whatever will most constructively handle the particular stress encountered.

Survival Responses allow you to flow along a continuum of many possible responses to stress. With well developed Survival Responses you can adapt to unexpected circumstances.

These skills are essential to manage the stresses of life.

Vision

Vitality

Courage

Resiliency

Sense of Humor

Reverence for Life

Spirit of Adventure

Cooperative Nature

Stress
Survival Skills

Survivors venture out into the world to face a mixture of surprises, struggles and challenges. The goal of stress management is to minimize pain and maximize pleasure.

These eight essential survival skills work in combination to assist during emergencies, help prevent distress and enrich the quality of life. Everyone has these skills to varying degrees. Which skills do you want to strengthen? What additional skills do you have to enhance your survival?

Vision
Survivors keep their attention clearly focused on their goals and priorities. They manage time and energy wisely. Some days they make bold leaps forward, other times taking small measured steps. Seeing the larger picture, they continue relentlessly forward. Their actions are guided from within without losing sight of the needs of others.

Vitality
Survivors create a lifestyle that produces an abundance of energy. Survivors maintain the vigor to thrive and face the demands of life. They schedule time to recharge batteries with exercise, recreation and supportive companionship. With strength of conviction, flexibility of mind and practiced endurance they are able to rise above struggles.

Courage
Survivors have the inner strength to act even when afraid. They have developed the insight to know when to be assertive and when to yield, forgive and let go. With self-confidence and determination, they question beliefs and confront unhealthy attitudes. They dare to act on their beliefs and are willing to adjust actions as necessary.

Resiliency

Survivors learn from their mistakes and bounce back. When faced with adversity they maintain a healthy attitude: "I will do whatever is needed to restore harmony." Survivors believe firmly that they can positively alter circumstances. They strive to prevent problems when possible and marshal a variety of resources to meet challenges. They develop problem solving skills that allow them to foresee new possibilities.

Sense of Humor

Survivors are playful and lighthearted, even daring to laugh at themselves. They derive pleasure from the simple joys of life and find fun in the most mundane of tasks. During difficult times, they maintain a healthy perspective. Even dealing with heavy issues, they appreciate the value of levity. Pleasure and creativity are priorities.

Reverence for Life

Survivors balance self-interest with respect for all life forms. Their personal convictions support and strengthen their will to live. They protect and nurture their self-esteem and inner peace. Compassion guides everyday actions. Survivors accept total responsibility for their well-being.

Spirit of Adventure

Survivors are enthusiastic and eager to ride in the front seat of the roller-coaster of life. They have a natural curiosity, a willingness to experiment, and a lifelong love of learning. Though they are risk-takers, they are not reckless. They seek both self-discovery and spiritual growth.

Cooperative Nature

Survivors are eager to work to achieve common goals. They can take leadership positions or follow directions when needed. Survivors offer assistance to friends and coworkers and can also ask for help. They can work alone when necessary but prefer teamwork. They seek solutions that serve the greater benefit of all.

52
Survival Tools

On the following pages are 52 Survival Tools that will guide you to healthy lifestyle changes one step at a time. Each tool enhances your use of the eight Stress Survival Skills.

Let each of these 52 tools become a healthy theme for one week. Throughout the year the 52 Stress Survival Tools will improve the overall skill and confidence with which you face the world. In no time at all, the simple act of scheduling moments for your weekly survival tool will become indispensible.

Tools includes title, illustrated text and suggested activities. Personalize activities by adapting them to your individual interests. The left hand page is for planning. Use your markers to color in the pictures.

Display this book in a prominent location to provide you with daily reminders. Approach each tool with a fresh attitude.

Sharing your Stress Survival Tools with family, friends and coworkers cuts the work in half and doubles the fun!

Set aside time each day to take good care of yourself.

Monday

Tuesday

Wednesday

Thursday

Friday

Saturday

Sunday

Wise Investments

Feeling like your emotional account is overdrawn? Are you living life on credit, making more withdrawals than deposits? Want to stop feeling emotionally bankrupt at the end of each day? Time to make wiser investments of time and energy?

Wasting $10 of energy on a $1 problem is a poor emotional investment. Failure to plan, overreacting or distress can result in a bad investment. To correct over investing, ask yourself: How much of my time and energy is necessary to deal with this problem? Learn to spend $1 worth of your time and energy on a $1 problem. Spend $10 only on a $10 problem.

Wise investors expend time and energy on things that yield a good return. They invest $1 and get $10 in return! When you invest your time wisely, you have a surplus of energy at the end of the day.

Each occasion that you handle money, check on your balance of time and energy:

Here are ways to make wise deposits into your emotional energy account.

- *Schedule time for exercise. This is always a high-yield activity.*

- *Take the time to prioritize your activities and commitments.*

- *Ensure quality time with friends.*

- *Schedule time for yourself. Do what you find most refreshing.*

- *Plan playtime.*

- *Identify the activities in your life that you consider your wisest investments.*

Monday

Tuesday

Wednesday

Thursday

Friday

Saturday

Sunday

Walks of Life

Walking is easy exercise. It benefits body, mind and spirit. A brisk walk clears the head and releases tension, leaving you feeling refreshed and energized. Regularly scheduled walks can keep you trim and improve both your cardiovascular system and your outlook on life. Everybody deserves to take the time for a daily walk.

Walking will always be one of the most popular fitness activities. All you need is a comfortable pair of shoes. Slow down and enjoy the beauty of your surroundings.

Explore a variety of walking opportunities.

• *Sunrise walks. Experience the beginning of a new day, the stirrings of the world coming to life. A slow, unhurried start will prepare you to handle the challenges ahead more effectively.*

• *Lunch walks. Add zest with a midday outing. Plan a picnic lunch at a park, fountain or square.*

• *Sunset walks. Climb to the top of a hill, mountain or ridge. Notice the slow change of the colors as the sun sets. Celebrate the transition from day to night.*

• *Night walks. Night walks are a wonderful way to end the day, providing time for reflection. Take note of the moon, the stars, the calmness of the night. Night walks ease you into a good night's sleep.*

Monday

Tuesday

Wednesday

Thursday

Friday

Saturday

Sunday

No Dumping!

No one would think of standing behind a dump-truck while it was unloading. Yet all too often we allow others to dump their emotional trash on us. Unwelcome emotional trash includes incessant complaints and criticisms. Dumpers may be feeling down in the dumps or have been dumped on by someone. And now they are trying to dump on you!

Be wary of the casual dumper who is constantly unloading small bundles on you. Or, you may know big dumpers who wait until they have a full load of trash and then plop. Being dumped upon by these people can feel like you've been hit by an avalanche.

Sometimes you realize you are only the innocent bystander who happens to be in the wrong place at the wrong time. It is time to prevent illegal dumping!

• *When you see someone coming toward you with a full load, get out of the way.*

• *Avoid dumping your trash on others. Anyone you dump on feels they have the right to dump on you in return.*

• *Communicate without feeling guilty that you are not available for dumps. "Sorry, no dumping."*

• *Practice saying to yourself: "No one has the right to dump on me."*

Monday

Tuesday

Wednesday

Thursday

Friday

Saturday

Sunday

Friends

"Friends are special people who encourage our growth, enrich our self-esteem, and by their presence give comfort."

Here are some ways to enjoy time with a friend.

• Contact an old friend from the past. Send a post card. Pick up the phone.

• Prepare breakfast-in-bed for a friend. Find out your friend's favorite treats and provide them.

• Schedule exercise time on a regular basis with a friend.

• Plan a monthly or bimonthly lunch date.

• Organize a surprise adventure for an old friend, new friend, mate, child or parent. Create a gift of quality time for you to share. Choose something that you both would enjoy doing. Plan an afternoon, entire day or a weekend block of time. Make all the arrangements, whether it be a picnic, camping trip or a night on the town. Tell your friend the kind of clothing to wear, the date and time he or she is to be ready for an adventure. You do the rest. The planning process itself can be great fun.

The joy of friendship comes from being with people you care about. Friends accept you as you are. Love, trust and honesty between friends bring out the best in the human spirit. Each friend can teach you something unique about yourself. Your selection of friends reflects your self-esteem.

Quality friendships require effort. You must be willing to invest both time and energy to create a shared history. Friends and fun go together.

Monday

Tuesday

Wednesday

Thursday

Friday

Saturday

Sunday

A Day of Rest

Imagine a 24 hour period of complete rest and relaxation – a day to call your own. Spend it how you want and where you want. Create a break from shoulds, oughts, musts and gottas. Plan a day void of responsibilities and pressures. Slow down and enjoy life the way you like it to be.

Do not wait until you get sick to take a day off. Sometimes people get sick and tired of never having time off. Recall the times you did become ill and the world did get by without you. One day of rest can prevent days of sickness. With a little planning, your day of rest can become a reality.

• *Take a well-day off from work. The point is to take an entire day for yourself with no excuses, no explanations; simply because you deserve it. Spend the day at home, in nature or anywhere you choose.*

• *When would be the best time to schedule your day? And how often? Once a week, once a month, once a season?*

• *What would you like to do on your day of rest? Exercise, read, play, sleep, hike, look at clouds, get some sun, do absolutely nothing? Consider spending a day in silence. Practice being completely lazy.*

• *Decide whether to spend your day alone or with a friend. If spending the time with children, make sure it is a time for playing.*

• *Exchange a day of rest with a mate, friend or parent. Take turns to free up the other person for their day of rest.*

Monday

Tuesday

Wednesday

Thursday

Friday

Saturday

Sunday

Crisis

In the Chinese language, the ideogram for "crisis" is a compound word composed of two parts: <u>danger</u> and <u>opportunity</u>. In Western culture, crisis is more commonly associated with only the danger aspect: pain, loss and even death. Crisis too often conjures up tragic images and feelings.

The ideogram points out that crisis also creates opportunities for dynamic personal growth. Every crisis presents the occasion to sharpen your crisis management skills. With practice you can become skilled both at seeing the hidden opportunities in a crisis and being aware of any danger.

First protect yourself from the danger. Then develop a crisis management strategy:

• *What can I learn from this crisis?*

• *How can I handle this challenge to strengthen my self-confidence?*

• *What adjustment in attitude or approach could help me bring this to resolution?*

• *What is a new way for me to handle this crisis?*

• *Would a sense of humor help me to discover the hidden opportunity in this crisis?*

• *What changes in approach or behavior would prevent the recurrence of this crisis?*

• *Do I need additional resources, counseling or skills? Where can I turn for help?*

Monday

Tuesday

Wednesday

Thursday

Friday

Saturday

Sunday

Do Your Feet a Favor

Feet are probably the most taken-for-granted part of your body. They get used and abused daily. They carry around a big load and are crammed into tight spaces. Your feet set the tone for the rest of the body. If they are cold, you feel cold. If your feet are tired, you feel tired.

Keep your feet comfortable so the rest of you feels great. Invest in comfortable footwear. Spend some time throughout the day with feet elevated to increase circulation. Try kicking your shoes off at different times.

In olden days, weary foot travelers would be welcomed at their destination with a foot washing ritual. Having walked for many miles, feet needed to be revived. Today, a foot washing ritual is a relaxing, caring activity to share with a friend. It invigorates the feet of the receiver and the hands of the giver! All you need is a large bowl, warm water, towel, soap, salt and lotion.

Your friend's feet will thank you from the bottom of their soles.

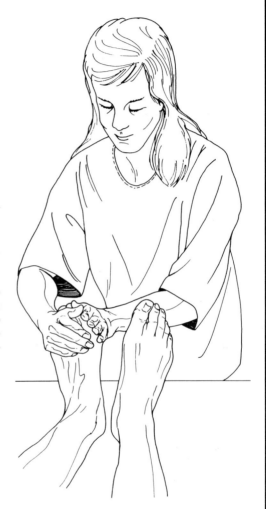

Foot Washing and Massage:

1. Create a relaxed and undisturbed atmosphere.

2. Soak the person's feet in a bowl of warm water.

3. Wash and massage the feet with soap.

4. While the feet are still wet, lightly rub with salt to cleanse and soften.

5. Rinse well afterward making sure to remove all remaining salt.

6. Dry the feet with a soft towel.

7. Apply lotion and massage each foot slowly.

Monday

Tuesday

Wednesday

Thursday

Friday

Saturday

Sunday

Cool It !

Since the beginning of time, water has been used to cleanse, heal, purify and refresh the spirit. In its varied forms, water provides a wealth of simple pleasures. Invigorate yourself by running your hands under a cold tap. Seek the soothing and relaxing pleasure of a warm shower or hot tub.

Before you reach burn-out, retreat to the calming comfort of water. Wash your cares down the drain. Seek out any occasions to hear, touch or bathe in the wonder of water. Water does the trick.

Try some of these watery delights:

bathe your pet

walk in the rain

soak in a hot tub

water your plants

squirt a water gun

shower with a friend

fling a water balloon

splash water on your face

drink a glass of cold water

wade in a mountain stream

gargle and make funny sounds

swim in a lake, river or ocean

indulge in a candlelight bath

run through a sprinkler

take a steambath

rest by a waterfall

play in a fountain

throw a snowball

soak your feet

Monday

Tuesday

Wednesday

Thursday

Friday

Saturday

Sunday

Get F.I.T.

For some people, it seems their exercise program consists of jumping to conclusions, pushing their luck, climbing the walls and dragging their heels. Others get even less exercise, and the excuses people make up for not exercising are hilarious. We all have our favorites.

Unfortunately, strenuous work is not always a substitute for good exercise. For exercise that brings you the most health benefit, look to the **F.I.T.** criteria:

Frequency—three times a week or
    more;
Intensity—challenging enough to
    raise your pulse, but not so
    strenuous that you are out of
    breath;
Time—15 minutes or more of
    continuous exercise per session.

Regular exercise has benefits for both body and spirit. Exercise helps your body to regulate appetite, burn stored fat and strengthen heart and lungs. Additionally, exercise can lower cholesterol and blood pressure. Physical activity clears the mind, improves sleep, helps to restore sense of humor and strengthens the will to live. Being fit generates the energy to live life to its fullest. Set aside time each day for exercise.

• *Record the frequency of your exercise on a calendar. Mark an X on the days that you do not exercise. Try to avoid 2 X's in a row.*

• *Compile a list of people with whom you can exercise and socialize.*

• *Reward yourself for following through on your commitment to become **F.I.T.***

Resource: *F.I.T.ness Game®*

Monday

Tuesday

Wednesday

Thursday

Friday

Saturday

Sunday

Letting Off Steam

Even the earth needs to let off steam sometimes. Volcanic eruptions, like the May 1980 eruption of Mount St. Helens, are devastating examples of what can happen when internal pressure is not released gradually.

For humans it is natural to feel anger, frustration, resentment and pain. These feelings exist for a reason and need to be expressed. The challenge is to learn how to release these pressures in constructive ways. If the pressure is correctly released, disaster can be avoided.

The body provides early warning signals that tension is starting to build, such as tight muscles or headaches. Practice releasing tension before a real eruption occurs.

Here are ground rules for letting off steam.

1. *Do not hurt yourself.*

2. *Do not hurt anyone else.*

3. *Do not hurt anything of value.*

4. *Reward yourself for releasing the pressure in a positive way.*

Creative pressure releases:

• *Hang a plastic milk jug from a string and hit with a stick.*

• *Tear up a cardboard box, old newspapers, catalogs or junk mail.*

• *Pound your bed with a pillow.*

• *Break up old clay flower pots or dishes before discarding.*

• *Yell, scream, rant and rave alone at home or at the car wash.*

Monday

Tuesday

Wednesday

Thursday

Friday

Saturday

Sunday

Your Special Spot

Think of a spot where you enjoy spending time. This special spot may be out in nature or even a room at home. It may be a place you know now or one you recall from childhood. Select any location that makes you feel comfortable and safe just thinking about being there.

During times of stress, take a five minute visit to this place, in your mind. This spot represents a private sanctuary for you, a healthy retreat from the pressures of life. Each time you visit, a wealth of new wonderful memories will be recorded.

Here are some ways to make good use of your special spot.

•   *Take a picture or purchase a postcard of your own special spot. Display it at home or work to remind you to take a relaxation break as needed. Close your eyes, take a few deep breaths and imagine that you are there. Let the image, the sounds and the smells of this place refresh and renew you.*

•   *Create a personal retreat space at home. It may be an unused room or favorite chair. Go there when you need a break.*

•   *Identify certain parks, fountains, scenic viewpoints or restaurants in your community to go to when you need a quick getaway.*

•   *Go back to your special spot as frequently as possible. Explore new places by sharing special spots with friends.*

Monday

Tuesday

Wednesday

Thursday

Friday

Saturday

Sunday

Play Ball !

As you grow older there is a tendency to play less and less. You spend most of your time doing "important" things. Yet, play remains a valuable way to rejuvenate the spirit. Ball games provide you with exciting and energetic ways to relieve tension, interact with friends and get exercise.

Think about how many different kinds of balls and ball games there are. Balls can be hit, thrown, kicked, swatted or bounced. Ball games provide unlimited opportunities to play. Round up the kids or your neighbors, yell "Play Ball" and let the season decide the ball game they choose.

Which of these ball games do you play? Which would you like to learn?

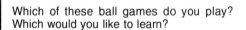

Baseball
Basketball
Golf
Football
Volleyball
Soccer
Bowling
Tennis
Racquetball
Handball
Ping Pong
Paddleball
Hackie Sack
Softball
Jacks
Beachball
Whiffleball
Superball
Mudball
Snowball

Monday

Tuesday

Wednesday

Thursday

Friday

Saturday

Sunday

Emotional Self-Defense

How well do you respond when people put you on the defensive, criticize your work or say things that hurt you? Emotional self-defense is the ability to shield yourself from the intentional and unintentional blaming and shaming that is directed your way.

Do you make yourself an easy target? Can you create a shield to protect yourself? Remember that people who are stressed out may attempt to take their pain out on you. It is possible to defend yourself without putting the other person on the defensive.

Learn to become a master in the art of emotional self-defense.

• *Emotionally distance yourself by not taking unwarranted criticism personally.*

• *Ask yourself if you are the actual target of the person's anger or did you just happen to be in their way.*

• *What percentage of the criticism do you consider valid? Separate fact from fiction; acknowledge what is true and throw out the rest.*

• *Shield yourself with a sense of humor.*

• *When necessary, give yourself permission to simply walk away.*

Monday

Tuesday

Wednesday

Thursday

Friday

Saturday

Sunday

Chocolate or Vanilla?

Sometimes you know exactly what flavor ice cream you want; other times a sample taste will help you decide.

You are constantly making decisions throughout the day. Some are a snap, while others feel more stressful. Too often decisions are made out of frustration, without thoroughly considering the consequences of either choice.

Prevent getting stuck with an option you dislike. Take the time to make a conscious choice. When important decisions need to be made, it is helpful to have a system that reduces confusion and anxiety.

To simplify the decision making process, follow these guidelines.

1. Narrow your decision down to the two best choices.

2. Allow the relative importance of the decision to determine the amount of time and energy you will invest exploring each choice.

3. Arbitrarily select one of the two choices and write out a list of the advantages and disadvantages. Then spend a period of time living with that choice.

4. Allow yourself an equal amount of time to live with the second option. Giving isolated time to each choice prevents the confusion of flipping back and forth between choices.

5. Having lived with and tasted both decisions for a while, ask yourself: Which feels like the best choice?

6. Act on your decision. If your choice continues to feel like the best option, great. If not, give yourself permission to change your mind. Remember you have not made a mistake, you are just learning from your actions. That is what life is all about.

Monday

Tuesday

Wednesday

Thursday

Friday

Saturday

Sunday

Just for the Fun of It

Do you impose a fun quota on yourself? Since no one lives forever, why are you working yourself to death? Do not hold back any longer. Spend time on the brighter side, nurturing your spirit of play and engaging your sense of humor. Play is the best cure for taking life too seriously. Let laughter, fun and frolic reflect your reverence for life.

This world can be one big playground, where all is absorbing and fascinating. Give yourself permission to be silly, foolish, expressive and impulsive. Send yourself out to play, and take a friend along. Fun is contagious. It is time to learn new ways to play.

Explore ways to turn work into play:

*   *Organize a good humor contest at work.*
*   *Do something outrageous–climb a tree, play with puppies, frolic in a pool.*
*   *Get out of your work clothes and into your play clothes.*
*   *Make funny faces, wear a silly hat, buy yourself a toy, learn a new game.*
*   *Make up your own "bumper snickers" for your car.*

*   *Create a Just For the Fun of It support group for people wanting to have more fun.*
*   *Wake up laughing, play under the covers, sing in the shower.*
*   *Spend time with funny friends.*
*   *Plan a surprise for a friend.*
*   *Post a list of ten things that you love to do to as a reminder to do them more regularly.*
*   *Add a new way to play each month.*

Monday

Tuesday

Wednesday

Thursday

Friday

Saturday

Sunday

In Case of Emergency

In any emergency, do not panic–stay calm. Take a deep breath, stop yourself from reacting rashly and begin exploring your choices. Select the best strategy.

Fight. *Be assertive, get your needs met.*

Flee. *Escape, remove yourself from the situation.*

Stay and play. *Engage sense of humor, laugh.*

Get physical. *Do not sit still; move your body. Walk, run, dance, jump.*

Ignore it. *Sometimes stress will go away if you do not give it too much attention.*

Take control. *Adjust attitude and make changes that give you power.*

Call for help. *Contact a friend or a professional so you do not have to continue alone.*

Slow down. *Many emergencies happen because you are going too fast.*

Goof off. *Space out, day dream, pretend.*

Retreat. *Vegetate, hibernate, become invisible. Take the day off.*

Get out of town. *Take a walk in a park, go to the woods, to the beach.*

Learn to say "no."

Break Glass.

Prevention is the best policy to minimize or eliminate illness, accidents and burn-out. But no matter how much you try to prevent them, not all emergencies can be avoided.

At any moment, personal emergencies can catch you off guard. Stress levels can reach alarming proportions. The best way to deal with these situations is to have an emergency procedure already in place.

Monday

Tuesday

Wednesday

Thursday

Friday

Saturday

Sunday

Slow Down

Faster. Hurry up. Now! Feeling rushed?

Are you taking on too many responsibilities? Are you expected to do twice as much work in half the amount of time? Overworked, pressured, feeling drained and driven to the point of exhaustion? Is your life a blur?

Responsibilities can not always be changed but they can be better balanced. Slow down. It's time to relax and recover. Establish a stable and peaceful space. Convert deadlines into finish lines. Repeat aloud: I did my best, now I will forget the rest.

- *Talk slowly. Walk slowly. Eat slowly.*

- *Take a nap each day.*

- *Each hour, schedule one minute just to sit and close eyes.*

- *Schedule lunch as a time to refuel and refresh.*

- *Organize your time and priorities better.*

- *Let go of unnecessary chores to make time for priorities.*

- *Practice doing one thing at a time and doing it well.*

- *Schedule a large block of time weekly for rejuvenation.*

- *Buy a pet turtle as a reminder to slow down.*

Monday

Tuesday

Wednesday

Thursday

Friday

Saturday

Sunday

Red
Yellow
Green Light

Traffic lights can be used as a reminder to check in on your level of stress throughout the day. The three colored lights can represent the levels of stress you may be experiencing. Red means distress, yellow signals caution and green suggests that it is safe to proceed. Ask yourself: "Which one of my lights is lit up now?"

Red
Are you in distress? Is the wear and tear of life greater than the amount of rest and repair? If so, the danger of an accident or illness is high. It is time to regroup, recharge and renew. Time to STOP on your own, before being stopped by disaster, disease or destruction. Ignoring a red light can set you up for a real crash!

Yellow
Is your body signaling you that something is wrong? Proceed with caution. Warnings may appear as muscular tension, headaches, irritability, sleep disturbances, accidents, forgetfulness or relationship problems. Time for concern.

Green
Feeling ready to go? Then it is safe to proceed. With stress at a healthy level, your life proceeds with balance and humor. You feel alive, alert, happy, relaxed, comfortable, energetic and enthusiastic. Life is good! Cruise on.

• *Monitor your stress level throughout each day. Practice observing the stress level of others.*

Monday

Tuesday

Wednesday

Thursday

Friday

Saturday

Sunday

Spring Blossom Courage

The courage of the crocus flower pushes forth its shoots through ground still blanketed with late snows. The plum tree blossoms at the earliest hint of spring even while the danger of late frost is still present. Witness the determination of last year's seed as it sprouts through the crack in the concrete. The quest for growth begins. Change is constant; courage is required.

Spring blossom courage is the ability to overcome uncertainty, obstacles and fear; to embrace life. This stirring within opens your heart to take risks, to blossom and seek growth in each experience. Some growth occurs naturally, but most must be cultivated. Instill confidence in yourself that you can make the best of the circumstances you encounter. Branch out in new directions. Let tree buds, flower bouquets and vegetable seedlings serve as reminders to open up and grow.

Create an optimal environment for inner growth through support and respect for your inner timing–the knowing when to act.

It takes courage to know when to begin relationships and when to end one and when it is time to move on.

It takes courage to ask for a promotion or look for a new job.

It takes courage to actively listen to someone whose views differ from yours.

It takes courage to accept the fact that children do not always turn out as parents would like them to.

It takes courage to let go of pain and seek love.

It takes courage to ask someone to dance.

Monday

Tuesday

Wednesday

Thursday

Friday

Saturday

Sunday

Vitamin T

Vitamin T is the nurturing nutrient found in healthy **Touch**. The US Department of Health and Happiness has established that Vitamin T is essential for every body. Natural sources of Vitamin T are handshakes, hugs, kisses, cuddles and rubs. Absorbed through the skin, this vitamin is obtained from family, friends and co-workers. One dose per hour yields an abundant supply. Megadoses are provided by massage. Positively habit-forming. No known megadose of this nutrient has ever been reported. Active ingredient: TLC (tender loving care.)

When applied topically, Vitamin T soothes the body, calms the mind, nourishes the spirit and warms the heart. Regular doses strengthen self-esteem, relieve stress and restore sense of humor...fast. Vitamin T also heals painful touches known as ouches (Touch — T = ouch). The main symptom of a Vitamin T deficiency is loneliness.

Guaranteed safe for all ages. Keep within reach of children. No artificial anything. Wholesome and non-caloric. Dispense with permission only.

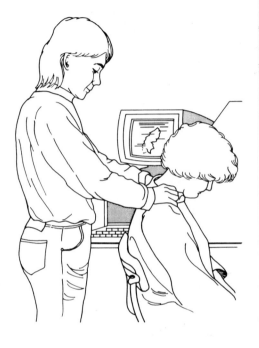

Give Vitamin T to friends and family.

•   *Do you have the Vitamin T you want?*

•   *Reach out to obtain an adequate daily supply of Vitamin T in the form of hugs, rubs and pats on the back.*

•   *Exchange Vitamin T with people of different ages, genders and cultures.*

•   *Eliminate all painful forms of touching such as put-downs, pokes, pushes and punches.*

Resource book:
    Vitamin T: A Guide to Healthy Touch

Monday

Tuesday

Wednesday

Thursday

Friday

Saturday

Sunday

Magic Star

Making changes and integrating them into your life is a constant challenge. Most changes are best made slowly and steadily, requiring some attention even on the busiest days. Like the string-on-the-finger, it is helpful to devise some method to help you remember the changes you intend.

Visual reminders provide a simple and easy way to keep your intentions focused. They help you give priority to the changes you want to make.

• *One type of reminder that works well is the small, self-adhesive stars placed in highly visible locations in your home. This simple technique is almost magical in how helpful it can be. Magic stars remind you to be conscious of decisions you have made: to play, breathe, relax, exercise or make other positive changes.*

• *Print the first letter of the word defining the change on the star. For example, if you want to relax more, write an "R".*

• *Place your magic star reminder on your watch, phone, mirror, dashboard, TV and refrigerator.*

• *Use this technique to assist you in carrying out other Survival Kit activities.*

Monday

Tuesday

Wednesday

Thursday

Friday

Saturday

Sunday

Your Daily Massage

Have you ever wished you had a live-in massage therapist? Well, you do, and it is you. While taking a shower, you can give yourself a mini-massage. Wash away stress and tension as you rub-a-dub-dub. Focus on selected tight muscle areas to give yourself a body refresher.

Your Daily Massage:

1. Give yourself a thorough head and scalp massage while shampooing your hair. Include your forehead and temples and do not forget your ears!

2. Lather hands with soap and knead needy muscles with firm pressure.

3. Massage your jaw muscles while washing your face.

4. Use your fingertips to massage tight neck and shoulder muscles.

5. Massage deeply into your stomach and hip muscles. Knead the long muscles of the thighs and calves.

6. If you have a shower partner, trade back massages. You will save water and have fun. Otherwise, use a back brush.

7. While rinsing, feel the soothing massaging action of the shower spray against your body. Imagine all your tension going down the drain.

8. Finish with a cool, energizing rinse. Continue your daily massage with a brisk towel rub. Pamper yourself with the application of powder, lotion or oil.

Monday

Tuesday

Wednesday

Thursday

Friday

Saturday

Sunday

Undercover Exercises

Undercover exercises are a gentle way to start your day. Performed in the warmth of your own bed, the exercises are designed to help you wake up, remove the kinks, and oxygenate your blood. Undercover exercises are to be done slowly while lying on your back. If you are feeling particularly stiff, you might choose to take a warm shower before doing the exercises.

You may also enjoy these undercover exercises at the end of the day to prepare for a good night's sleep. Release lingering tensions as you stretch and breathe.

1. *Rotate your head from side to side.*
2. *Rotate your eyes first left, then right. Squint and then relax.*
3. *Tighten then relax the muscles of your face.*
4. *Wrap your arms around one knee and bring it in toward your chest. Breathe while relaxing your lower back. Repeat with other knee.*
5. *Now draw both knees to your chest, rotating your ankles in ever-widening circles.*
6. *With your arms up in the air, rotate your wrists slowly.*
7. *Extend your arms above your head one at a time and then both together.*
8. *Stretch your legs one at a time. Flex and point your toes while gently holding the stretch.*
9. *Do a diagonal stretch, extending right arm and left leg; then left arm and right leg.*
10. *Wrap your left arm around your right shoulder. Wrap your right arm around your left shoulder. Give yourself a big hug.*

Monday

Tuesday

Wednesday

Thursday

Friday

Saturday

Sunday

Time Out

Time out gives you an opportunity to adjust your attitude, develop a new perspective and choose a healthy response.

Practice emotional self-defense

Take a deep breath

Close your eyes

Take a shower

Let off steam

Call a friend

Take a walk

Slow down

Swim laps

Play ball

Go wild

Play

On the playing field, the referee calls a "time out" to stop the action when there has been a foul or an injury. The coach may also call for time out when too many mistakes are being made, when players need to rest or in order to plan a new strategy.

In the great game of life, you are the official in charge and can decide when to take your own time out. About to say something that might hurt someone's feelings? Stop for a time out. On the verge of losing your temper with your child? Time out! When rushed and in danger of making costly mistakes at work, call for a time out. At the end of a hard day, exhausted from the avalanche of problems you had to face, take a time out.

Monday

Tuesday

Wednesday

Thursday

Friday

Saturday

Sunday

Public Enemy #1

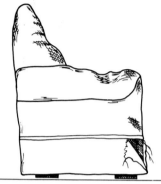

PUBLIC ENEMY #1
65758595

PUBLIC ENEMY #1
65758595

Wanted by the FBI.
Name: Louie the Lounger. Aliases: Charlie the Chair, Bernie the Barstool, Ronnie Recliner.

Description
Height: 3 feet.
Age: unknown.
Weight: 25 lbs. avg.
Race: multi-colored.
Complexion: leathery.
Build: medium to large.
Distinguishing Marks: signs of wear on
  bottom.

Criminal Record
Though quiet and soft-spoken, Louie is frequently accompanied by a loud, and unruly partner, The Tube. His apprehension is also being sought for disturbing the peace. Louie has been convicted of seducing victims into sedentary lifestyles. He is notorious for boredom, lethargy, laziness and escape.

Caution
Louie the Lounger should be considered armed and dangerous. Avoid contact.

If you have information concerning this culprit, please contact the FBI office:

> J. Edgar Mover, Director
> Federal Bureau of Intervention
> Washington D.C. 2000l

• *Make important life decisions while walking.*

• *When you need to relax, lay down and take a nap.*

• *Schedule a walk-and-talk with friends and colleagues.*

• *Design work area to allow movement.*

> *"The mind can not absorb what the behind can not endure."*

Monday

Tuesday

Wednesday

Thursday

Friday

Saturday

Sunday

So What!

A guaranteed formula for burn-out is to take on responsibility for everything and everybody. Focusing on other people's problems will leave you with little time to do what you want to do. Before you burn up completely, repeat this simple phrase: "So What?" Ask yourself, "How important is this? Is it my responsibility? Will it matter a week or a month from now? Is this worth endangering my health?"

So What if I don't cut the grass today! So What if the book shelves need dusting! So What if I make speling mistakes! So what! is a constructive stress management response when you find yourself overcommitted, overstressed and overwhelmed. When appropriate, practice healthy indifference.

Review the activities that fill your day:

* *List activities that are most important to you.*

* *Do one activity at a time.*

* *Stop wasting energy worrying about what you did not get done.*

* *Put up a sign saying "So What!" as a reminder to stay sane.*

* *Prioritize tasks in this way:*
  A. Things that need to be done today
  B. Things that can be done tomorrow
  C. Things that can be done whenever.

  Rest and start fresh tomorrow.

Monday

Tuesday

Wednesday

Thursday

Friday

Saturday

Sunday

Listen

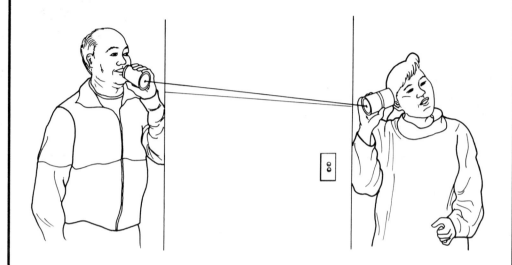

Communication does not occur when two people are talking and neither is listening. Too frequently people cut each other off in mid-sentence, being overly anxious to express their own point of view. Have you ever witnessed a ping-pong conversation with two people talking back and forth so rapidly that neither hears? Or have you tried speaking with someone who is so busy rehearsing what to say next that he or she fails to listen to you?

There are times when you want someone to just listen. Good listeners are attentive and sympathetic. They are interested in what you have to say and the uniqueness of your point of view. Enhance your communication skills by taking turns, one person talking and one person listening.

Practice listening with your heart, not just with your head.

Listen to the words. Then listen again to the intention behind the words.

Listen, demonstrating full attention by making eye contact, facing the speaker directly and acknowledging gestures.

Listen without interruption, judgement or advice.

Listen and ask questions to clarify meanings.

Listen and paraphrase to assure understanding.

Listen. Soon it will be your turn.

Monday

Tuesday

Wednesday

Thursday

Friday

Saturday

Sunday

Enriching
Self-Esteem

Self-esteem is the honor and respect you give yourself. Your self-esteem needs to be based on a realistic belief in your capabilities. Your level of esteem influences all of your thoughts, feelings and actions. In essence, the quality of the relationship you have with yourself directly affects the quality of the relationships you have with others!

A strong self-esteem provides the best defense against distress. When you feel good about yourself, you tend to interpret events and interactions positively. Protect your self-esteem; it is your most valuable possession. Fill your life with activities that enrich your own and others' self-worth.

Self-esteem is being a good friend to yourself.

• *Write a letter to yourself as if you were writing a letter praising the qualities of a best friend. Mention the special qualities, talents, skills and personal characteristics you value.*

• *Make a scrapbook of photos of yourself from infancy to present day as a reminder of your growth and changes.*

• *Plan your birthday as an occasion to celebrate your existence.*

• *Schedule time for exercise, rest, friends and fun to demonstrate your commitment to self-esteem.*

Monday

Tuesday

Wednesday

Thursday

Friday

Saturday

Sunday

Teamwork

On the late night news, a group of survivors from a recent plane crash described their ordeal. Beyond radio contact and with several injuries, they struggled to fight off panic. They realized that their survival depended upon working together. After three strenuous days, they emerged as a team, glad to be alive!

When feeling lost, overwhelmed or distressed, it is time to reach out for support. Assemble a support team.

In an effective team, each member assumes responsibility for the desired result. Teamwork requires flexibility, being able to both follow directions and assume a leadership role. Openness to others' ideas and problem solving approaches strengthens the team. Teamwork gets the job done with each member feeling good about the process, themselves and each other.

Let teamwork reduce distress and increase the satisfaction in everyday struggles.

* *Be on the lookout for opportunities to create and work together as a team.*
* *Look for projects that you typically do alone and ask for help.*
* *Ask friends to help expand your social contacts by introducing you to their friends.*
* *Team up with other couples to discuss relationship issues.*

* *Join a support group.*
* *Organize groups to help solve community problems.*
* *Convert deadlines into finish lines at work, with everyone crossing together as winners.*
* *Work smart. Work as a team.*

Monday

Tuesday

Wednesday

Thursday

Friday

Saturday

Sunday

Stress Ball

Humans have been throwing their anger, pain and aggression at each other since time began. Kids throw mudballs, snowballs and spitballs. Maybe there is a natural human need to throw things. Unfortunately, it can hurt someone, causing more stress than it relieves.

Any soft foam ball makes a great stress ball. Relieve stress by throwing it against a wall. Do not hold stress inside. You become stronger when you let stress out in healthy ways. So stand up and give it your best shot!

When you feel:

ready to explode. . . . . hit it

stomped on by life. . . . . kick it

like you're losing it. . . . . hold it

too much responsibility. . . . . drop it

feeling lonely and rejected . love it

tired of putting up with it . . . . sit on it

tossed around. . . . . juggle it

up against the wall. . . . . bounce it

you're losing your grip. . . . . squeeze it.

Monday

Tuesday

Wednesday

Thursday

Friday

Saturday

Sunday

Deep Breathing

When your body is tense, your breath frequently becomes shallow. This response to tension can create disease.

Deep breathing is one of the simplest and best techniques for managing stress. You cannot remove certain pressures from your life, but you can control your reaction to them. Deep breathing reduces muscle tension and emotional fatigue and clears the mind. Inhaling large amounts of oxygen nourishes body cells while increasing energy, concentration, alertness and creativity.

• **Practice deep breathing.** *While seated or lying down, inhale slowly through the nose. Feel the stomach rise, chest expand and shoulders raise as air completely fills the lungs. Exhale slowly and deeply, squeezing in the stomach muscles to release all residual air. Stop if you begin to feel light-headed. Take a few normal breaths and then return to deep breathing.*

• **Breathe to ten.** *Whenever you realize you are getting upset or stressed-out, take ten deep breaths. Relax and let go of the tension with each exhale.*

• **Breathe stickers.** *Create reminders that help you remember to breathe and relax throughout the day. Stick them up on your speedometer, phone, mirror or file cabinet. Breathe deeply, slow down and relax.*

Monday

Tuesday

Wednesday

Thursday

Friday

Saturday

Sunday

Burn It

Is there too much junk in your life? Does your house contain reminders of your past which you have outgrown? Do you still have those ugly drapes? Is there furniture you hate? Give your home a spring cleaning. Gather up the things that are gathering dust and donate them to your favorite charity.

Destroy all the photographs of yourself you wish had never been taken. Recycle those old clothes that no longer fit your personality.

Do recurring negative thoughts and feelings cling to your mind like gum on a shag carpet? Does the mental clutter of unpleasant memories keep you frozen in the past? Are you holding on to grudges? Do you belittle yourself for past mistakes? Unburden yourself from lingering regrets. Empower yourself by making space in your mind for more positive and productive thoughts.

The following fire ritual may help to free yourself from the burdens of the past.

1. Collect all the burnable objects you want to remove from your life.

2. Take them to a burning site, such as a fireplace, woodstove, barbecue grill or campfire.

3. Then write out a short description of the thoughts, memories and feelings you do not want to have anymore either.

4. Carefully build your fire.

5. As you place each object or written reminder into the fire, watch the past be consumed.

Monday

Tuesday

Wednesday

Thursday

Friday

Saturday

Sunday

Pleasant Dreams

The quality of your sleep relates to the kind of day you have had. A day that is rushed, plagued by deadlines and long working hours is a setup for a restless night. Anxious days lead to anxious nights with sleep that fails to refresh. A good night's sleep is the best preparation for the challenges of the coming day.

Sound sleep does not happen by accident. Good nutrition, exercise and periods of relaxation lead to deeper sleep. Finish your day on a peaceful note.

Lead yourself gently into dreamland. Let the fun continue while you are asleep. Pleasant dreams.

Creating a relaxed evening routine will improve your chances of pleasant dreams.

take a warm bath

read a good book

prepare for the next day

exchange back rubs

play your favorite music

take an evening walk

Monday

Tuesday

Wednesday

Thursday

Friday

Saturday

Sunday

Time Well Spent

Is your time well spent? Stop for a moment and think about the activities that fill your day. Certain activities energize you, leaving you more excited about life. Others drain you. The goal is to fill your day with more of the energizing activities that enhance your vitality.

Make sure you take frequent breaks and ask yourself: "How well am I spending my time? What can I do to refresh myself at this moment? What needs and goals can I hope to meet before this day ends?"

- *Fill your life with more meaningful challenges.*

- *Identify the skills you need to do your work more efficiently.*

- *Bring your work in line with your higher values.*

- *Build supportive routines and friendships.*

- *Express your unique interests and talents daily.*

- *Take time to energize yourself through exercise and relaxation.*

- *Eliminate one way that you waste time.*

- *Begin a be-sure-to-do list of daily activities that are most important to you.*

- *Ask yourself: Am I enjoying life? Is my time well spent?*

Resource book: Time Well Spent

Monday

Tuesday

Wednesday

Thursday

Friday

Saturday

Sunday

Feathered Friends

Are you feeling surrounded by turkeys when you would rather be soaring with eagles? When you feel weighted down by everyday living, let the sight of your feathered friends uplift your spirit. If you are feeling caged, let the flight of a bird bring inspiration to plan your escape. When the song is gone from your heart, whistle along with a bird.

The joys of birdwatching are available whenever you take the time to notice. Experience the playfulness of a meadowlark as it dips and dives to catch its morning meal. Enjoy the grace and adaptability of ducks one moment in flight and the next moment swimming beneath the water. Let the annual return of the swallows remind you of the many mysteries of life. Revel in the palette of colors on a mallard's back. Study the intricacies of nest building. Enjoy the songs of birds beginning their day as you depart for work. Birding is readily available as a hobby or simple pleasure.

- *Place a birdfeeder outside your kitchen window.*

- *Build a birdhouse to welcome a favorite bird back to your neighborhood.*

- *List the birds you see with the help of a regional bird identification book.*

- *Include your bird book on hikes or vacations.*

- *Bring binoculars for a bird's eye view.*

- *Start a feather collection*

- *Attend birding activities of local nature organizations.*

- *Schedule a zoo trip to view birds from around the world.*

- *Learn to recognize bird songs.*

- *Feed the ducks.*

- *Experience flight first-hand in a glider, parachute or small plane.*

Monday

Tuesday

Wednesday

Thursday

Friday

Saturday

Sunday

Seasons

Does it sometimes seem that life is going too fast? You are working so hard that one day it is winter and the next time you look summer is already here. Too busy, you missed the beauty of another spring.

Eliminate the blur. Celebrate the passage of time, allowing each moment to become clear and full of details. Be like a seasonal barometer, taking time to notice the changes in your world.

Plan some outside time daily to enjoy the beauty of spring, summer, fall and winter. Observe both subtle and dynamic changes of nature's cycle. Schedule seasonal rituals to celebrate winter and summer solstice as well as spring and fall equinox.

Slow down and appreciate your world.

•   *Choose one tree that you can observe as it cycles from new buds to bare limbs.*

•   *Note the quality of light and the shift in time and position of the rising and setting sun.*

•   *Do your moods vary with the seasons?*

•   *When are you first aware of the changing quality of the air heralding the arrival of each season?*

•   *Listen to outside chimes as they signal the changes of the wind through the seasons.*

•   *What month of the year are you most likely to see rainbows, hear lightning and feel the hardest rain?*

•   *Which outdoor activities do you look forward to each season?*

•   *Prepare special foods that are symbolic of each season.*

Monday

Tuesday

Wednesday

Thursday

Friday

Saturday

Sunday

Dance for Joy

Dance is one of the oldest forms of creative expression. Before writing was invented, people danced to describe events and feelings as well as to celebrate rituals and rites of passage.

Dance creates a natural outlet for joys and sorrows. The rhythmic movement of the body to music provides an expressive release for stress and tension. Besides being great physical exercise, dancing yields an opportunity to meet new friends. Celebrate the simple joy of being fully alive with dance.

Enjoy dance with a group or as a private activity, on a dance floor or in your living room. Find the right music and movement for you. Choose from ballet, jazz, modern, tap, square, folk, disco, ballroom, belly, swing, aerobic and ethnic dance.

- *Select a new dance form to learn.*

- *Join a dance group that provides ongoing instruction.*

- *Throw a dance party, inviting friends to bring their favorite dance music.*

- *Dance with people of all ages.*

- *Seek out music to match your mood.*

- *Experience the feeling of dancing until you are completely exhausted.*

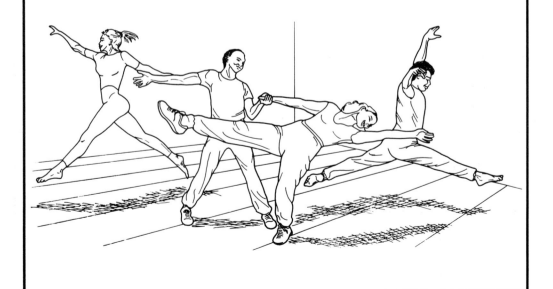

Monday

Tuesday

Wednesday

Thursday

Friday

Saturday

Sunday

Wellness for Life

There are two groups of risk factors contributing to premature death. One group is beyond your control. Examples include gender, genetics and accidents. The other risk factor group, however, is within your control. It includes lifestyle, behavior and attitudes.

Wellness is a way of life to achieve your highest level of health and happiness. Create opportunities to develop your whole self: body, mind, spirit. Invest your time, energy and money to acquire healthy habits. Your attitude and actions reflect your self-esteem.

Wellness is made up of physical, spiritual, mental, emotional, social, economic and environmental health. Changes occur in small increments. The path to wellness is a lifelong journey; make every step enjoyable.

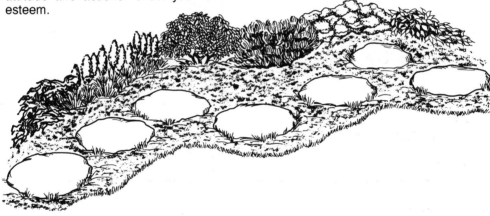

Pick one of the seven areas of health. Make a commitment to move awareness into action.

• *Write out an action plan, stating clearly what you want to change and how you will begin.*

• *How can you derive encouragement from friends?*

• *What resources, skills and information will assist you?*

• *Consider how you can anticipate obstacles plus strengthen your motivation to be successful in this goal.*

• *Determine how you will record and reward progress.*

• *How can you help friends on their paths to wellness?*

Monday

Tuesday

Wednesday

Thursday

Friday

Saturday

Sunday

Playtime

Has life become boring? You can tell you are overworked when you do not have time to play. Step out of your world of responsibility and career and step into the world of a child. Let time with a child be a refresher course in fun, imagination and laughter. Fantasy time is when anything is possible. Treat yourself with a reprieve from mature, adult behavior to balance your life with play.

Kids are the masters of play, and would love to remind you how. Let the child be your tour guide. Be silly, play in the grass, color outside the lines. Show children that adults can still have fun. Play for play's sake. Enjoy the timelessness of a child's pleasures. Enhance the child's self-esteem through shared playtime. Let your actions say: "I think you are so special. I want to be with you and do what you want to do." This message is the key into the child's world.

Take a break from the real world.

• *Schedule time with children of different ages and gender.*

• *Play with your own child or borrow a child from a relative or friend.*

• *Choose activities the child loves.*

• *Begin with small periods of time, moving up to a full day.*

• *Play follow the leader. Let the child plan the activities as you follow along.*

• *Play ball until the child wants to stop.*

• *Eat what, how and when the child wants to eat.*

• *Lie on the floor and ask the child to tell you a story.*

• *Consider becoming a Big Brother or Big Sister.*

Monday

Tuesday

Wednesday

Thursday

Friday

Saturday

Sunday

Back to Nature

Get away from your normal routines. Hide your watch and go on Outdoor Standard Time. Adjust to the rhythms of nature. Eat when hungry, rest when tired. Step into the world of nature: it may be as close as your own back yard.

Respectfully observe wildlife in natural settings. Seek a fresh perspective where the air is clear. Go back to nature to reconnect with the beauty and oneness of life.

Give yourself a daily dose of nature in your own backyard or nearby park. Make plans to explore new areas.

• *Spend time in the parks or gardens in your community.*

• *Explore recreational opportunities available in neighboring streams, lakes or rivers.*

• *Refresh your body, mind and spirit with a hike in the woods.*

• *Enjoy a bike ride through local orchards, farmlands, meadows or wilderness areas.*

• *Plan weekend campout adventures: back-packing, car or van camping. State and national park maps provide information on hiking trails, camping spots, sanitation facilities, elevation, etc.*

• *Learn new ways of enjoying time out in nature: bird-watching, wildflower identification, mushrooming, wildlife photography, canoeing or cross-country skiing.*

• *Become a picnic expert by eating as many meals as possible out of doors. The atmosphere is great and the appetite is hearty.*

• *Join a group that organizes hikes, camping trips, canoe outings and other nature-based events.*

• *Treat yourself to a daypack or hiking boots. Give outdoor gear as gifts to friends.*

Monday

Tuesday

Wednesday

Thursday

Friday

Saturday

Sunday

Thanks

Having a bad day? Is everything going wrong? Remind yourself, attitude is everything. Obsessing on your troubles can make them worse. Just for fun, consider being thankful for things that did not go wrong. Giving thanks for all that you have keeps your life in healthy perspective. Regardless of what goes wrong, you can still be grateful for all that goes right.

Give thanks every day. If you have food to eat and clothes to wear you are doing well. You may not always like your job, but at least you have one. There is so much to be thankful for. By shifting your focus to the positive aspects, you can brighten up your day and the day of those around you. Express your appreciation to those people who help you see the brighter side of life.

Try some of these ways of being thankful.

*   *With each meal, practice giving thanks to the earth for the food available to you.*

*   *In the morning, give thanks for being alive. In the evening, review all that went well, the special events that brought pleasure.*

*   *Spend time reflecting on the friends and family who enrich you. Express your appreciation. Thank them for enhancing the quality of your life.*

*   *Acknowledge the material goods that add efficiency and comfort: the hot shower that starts your day or the computer that eases your work.*

*   *Most important of all is to be thankful for who you are.*

Monday

Tuesday

Wednesday

Thursday

Friday

Saturday

Sunday

Wish List

When life seems to be an endless list of things that you have to do, it's time to balance with a wish list of things you want to do. What do you wish for when you blow out birthday candles, throw a coin in the fountain or pull apart a wishbone? Do you still make a wish on the evening star?

Wishes come true in many forms: buying new clothes, learning to play the piano, traveling to a location you have always dreamed of. Wishing is like dreaming; anything can come true. When making a wish, give your imagination free rein without the limitation of "impossible thinking." Learn to recognize and appreciate the wishes that have been fulfilled. You have the power to make more wishes come true. Dare to ask for what you want.

• Write out a list of all the things that you would like to have come true. Include small, medium and large wishes. List both immediate and long range wishes. Some wishes may come into your life as gifts while others require a plan to make your dreams come true. After you have made your list, place a mark by the items you are most willing to work toward.

• Post your list and ask for support from friends and family.

• As your wishes are fulfilled, check them off.

• Keep adding to your list.

• While pursuing your dreams, learn to value the journey as much as the fulfillment.

• If your wishes are not coming true, reflect upon how to remove the obstacles to their fulfillment.

• Keep your dreams alive.

Monday

Tuesday

Wednesday

Thursday

Friday

Saturday

Sunday

Give To The Earth

Mother Earth is not a happy planet. Drinking polluted water, breathing unclean air and eating contaminated food causes you distress. This distress is of such proportions that humans are now on the list of endangered species. Earth remains the only planet known of in the universe that can support life. But the Earth has its limits. As the population continues to swell, each of us must learn to replenish the earth.

You share the world in interdependence with thousands of other forms of life. Stem the tide of pollution, the misuse of resources and the extinction of more species. As an informed consumer, you can learn to make environmentally sound choices. Take steps to become a better caretaker of your planet. Only conscious lifestyle choices can ensure survival.

• *There is no longer anything we can afford to throw away. Once is not enough! Refill. Return. Repair. Rebuild. Reclaim. Recharge. Rethink. Reduce. Reuse. Recycle.*

• *Gardening brings awareness to the importance of the quality of the planet's topsoil. Compost or plant a cover crop to improve the soil. Watch things grow. Feel the soil with fingers and toes, and eat the fruits of your labor. When you give to the Earth, Earth returns the bounty.*

• *Plant trees. They provide the earth with oxygen from photosynthesis, remove pollution from the air and cool the planet.*

• *Every living thing depends upon water. Take action at home and work to preserve the purity of fresh and salt water.*

Monday

Tuesday

Wednesday

Thursday

Friday

Saturday

Sunday

Your Best With Grace

Do you have photographs of yourself as you took your first baby steps? To help you get started, parents held your hands and guided you through your initial movements. You fell dozens of times, but got up again and again until finally you could walk across the room. In no time at all, you were running throughout the house.

As adults, we often judge first efforts too harshly. We become overly concerned with doing things "right" or "perfect" on the first attempt. Learning involves being willing to risk making mistakes. Be gentle with yourself when learning new steps. Take pride in your determination during periods of exploration.

In doing your best with grace, you return to that sense of adventure you felt as child. Learning is undertaken with a blend of playfulness and compassion. Do your best, knowing that you will improve with time. See learning as a journey of self-discovery.

• *Give yourself permission to make mistakes. Stretch your limits. Do not let mistakes be a drain on your self-worth. Ask yourself: What can I learn from these mistakes?*

• *Avoid comparing your abilities to anyone else's. Respect each person's abilities and efforts as you respect your own. Give grace to yourself and others.*

• *Purposefully place yourself in new situations on a regular basis. Enjoy the fresh vision of a beginner. Find pleasure in watching improvement happen over time.*

• *Select times when you choose to do your best. Find other occasions when half best will do.*

• *Practice positive affirmations:*

> *"I am doing my best with grace."*

> *"My best is good enough."*

> *"I will be the best I can be."*

Monday

Tuesday

Wednesday

Thursday

Friday

Saturday

Sunday

Vision Fitness

When you overexert your eyes, both mind and body will feel the strain. Your eyes need to be kept physically fit for optimal performance. The muscles that move the eyes need to be stretched, relaxed and strengthened. When you reduce wear and tear on your eyes, you reduce stress on your mind. Keep your eyes in good shape through proper use and rest.

• Ensure proper lighting with natural or full-spectrum light. Avoid fluorescent light. Maintain adequate lighting while reading.

• Reduce glare. Wear quality sunglasses while driving or in direct sun.

• Practice "zooming." Use your eyes like a camera lens: look at something up close and then zoom into the distance. Repeat several times. Avoid staring.

• Take frequent eye breaks. Each hour, give your eyes a 3-5 minute rest by closing them. When you close your eyes your brain slows. Blink every few seconds to allow your eyes to be moistened.

• Stretch. Take your eyes through a full range of motion, slowly and without straining. Look up and down, left to right; rotate clockwise and counterclockwise. Remember to breathe deeply. Squeeze your eyes shut, then relax and open them.

• Enjoy 40 winks. Consider taking a 10 - 20 minute nap to rest your eyes as well as your whole body.

• With eyes closed, massage around your eye sockets, forehead and temples. Smooth the skin above the eyebrows. Gently press down on the eyeballs themselves.

Monday

Tuesday

Wednesday

Thursday

Friday

Saturday

Sunday

E.A.T.

Does eating stress you out? Are you worried about the fat content of every potato chip? Captivated by every diet you read about? Do you suffer from nutritional nightmares, imagining that the foods you eat are out to get you? In this era of junk food and health fads the simple act of eating can become a burden to daily peace of mind.

Now is the time to lighten up and learn to treat food as a friend. And the best way to have a good relationship with food is to eat consciously and enjoy. You can make eating both pleasurable and healthy. By maintaining the simple guidelines of **E.A.T** (**E**ating **A**wareness **T**raining), you can learn to relish the simple pleasures of food.

E.A.T. Guidelines:

•   *During one or more meals each day, slow down and enjoy every mouthful.*

•   *Relish the preparation of a meal: the textures, smells, colors and final arrangement of the food.*

•   *Whether at home, in a restaurant or at a picnic, make meals a special time together with friends and family.*

•   *Savor your favorite foods and allow them to melt slowly in your mouth.*

•   *Follow the 90/10% rule: 90% of your food for health and 10% of your food for recreation.*

Monday

Tuesday

Wednesday

Thursday

Friday

Saturday

Sunday

The Quest

Integral to many cultures is a rite of passage called the vision quest. The quest consists of time spent alone in nature. It is a concentrated period of time to reflect on the direction and purpose of one's life.

Spending time alone to clarify your life path can be a beacon to help you direct your time and effort. You can learn to avoid aimless wandering and eliminate mindless distractions. A quest can help you focus and move forward toward your life goals. Take time to attune to yourself and your innermost thoughts. Enjoy time to be one with nature and the forces of the universe.

- *Set aside a period of time free from normal activities. You may consider doing this quest by yourself or with a special friend.*

- *Select a location of personal significance for your retreat. Quest opportunities may arise while camping, attending an organized retreat, spending time at a favorite resort or in the privacy of your own home.*

- *Examine who you are now and who you want to become. Are you allowing anything to keep you from your path?*

- *Ask yourself what you want to do with your life. Record your thoughts, feelings and goals.*

- *After your quest is over, select a memento of the experience to keep the memory of the quest alive.*

Monday

Tuesday

Wednesday

Thursday

Friday

Saturday

Sunday

Go Wild !

Humans spend the vast majority of their time being exceedingly civilized and tame. Constantly trying to be sane can drive you insane. You can feel trapped in situations where you can neither fight nor flee. Watching people act wildly on television and movie screens is no substitute for the real thing.

Well, it's time to let your wild side be expressed. Jump, yell, scream and dance. In the heart of each person is a wild and untamed animal wanting to be set free. Remember, you can go wild without endangering yourself or others. Decide which activities would be wild for you.

The wild person within seeks a safe outlet.

*   *Go wild! Get fit. Kayak, climb mountains, windsurf, ski. Experience the exhilaration of controlled risk.*

*   *Go wild! Build a campfire, hunt, fish, dine on wild berries, swim naked in a pond. Dress in primitive attire. Sense kinship with the other wild creatures of the world.*

*   *Go wild! Play out in the rain, climb a tree, walk barefoot, run wildly through the woods.*

*   *Go wild! Let loose dancing. Express strong feelings. Be outrageous. Do something that would surprise your friends, and maybe yourself. Allow your spirit of adventure to take over. Be creative.*

*   *Go wild! Discover new ways to bring wildness to your workplace — without getting fired!*

Monday

Tuesday

Wednesday

Thursday

Friday

Saturday

Sunday

Do Not Disturb

Is there a constant barrage of noise in your life? Are you rudely awakened by the racket of garbage trucks or the roar of traffic? Are you plagued by unwanted phone interruptions? Does your car have an irritating buzz that no amount of money can locate? Is there a whining voice that grates on your nerves? Is a nauseating commercial jingle rattling incessantly through your brain? Are you ready for some peace and quiet?

Hang out the Do Not Disturb sign. Take time to relax and be still. Quiet at night is not enough; the body needs quiet periods in the daytime. Defend yourself from the invasion of the noisy intruders.

•   *Schedule time when you are not to be disturbed.*

•   *Remove as many sounds as possible: phone, TV, radio and traffic.*

•   *Purchase ear plugs or screen out sounds with background music.*

•   *Spend a period of time being quiet, speaking only when necessary. For example, enjoy one meal each week in complete silence.*

•   *Arrange time in nature where the few sounds you do hear are pleasant to the ear.*

Monday

Tuesday

Wednesday

Thursday

Friday

Saturday

Sunday

I Will

Do you have your life in order? Have you made your last wishes known? There are two types of will that can allow you to participate in the important decisions of your final days. A Living Will addresses difficult health care decisions if you were to become terminally ill. The Last Will and Testament specifies your personal wishes regarding the handling of your remains and the type of ceremony or ritual you would prefer. Wills also address how your estate will be managed.

At an early age you realized that you would not live forever. Yet there is a tendency to live under the illusion that there is always plenty of time. There are no guarantees.

What is important for you to do before you die?

• Take an afternoon stroll in a local cemetery. While walking, ponder the question: What would I do if I only had one day, one week, one month or one year left to live.

Words of wisdom from the mouth of a five year old:

"From now on I will live everyday until I die."

Monday

Tuesday

Wednesday

Thursday

Friday

Saturday

Sunday

Prescription for Awful-izing

Have things been going too well lately? Do you need relief from happiness? Missing pain, suffering and the sympathy you used to receive? Here is a prescription guaranteed to make you feel miserable fast.

Blame others for how you feel. When you feel hurt, angry or upset make sure to let others know it's all their fault. Make them feel guilty.

"Should" on yourself. Constantly tell yourself what you should and should not do.

Be critical. Criticize everything about yourself starting with your looks. Then begin nagging at friends and family.

Be a people-pleaser. Remind yourself that other people's wants and needs come first. Always put yourself last.

Be perfect. Never make a mistake or do anything wrong. If you do err, call yourself "stupid" and keep striving for perfection.

Yes, but . . . Always have plenty of excuses for why you can not do what you would like to do.

If only . . . When anything bad happens, tell yourself that somehow it is totally your fault.

I can't . . . Act helpless. Never forget that you have absolutely no control over your life.

Put yourself down. Remind yourself that you are untalented and unlovable. Belittle yourself and take no pride in any of your accomplishments.

Be a martyr. Assume responsibility for everyone's feelings and if they do not appreciate all you have done for them, be resentful.

Monday

Tuesday

Wednesday

Thursday

Friday

Saturday

Sunday

Last, but not Least

What thoughts, memories and inspirations have guided you? Create your own stress survival tools. Summarize your idea in one or two paragraphs. Then describe the illustration that will be able to evoke these thoughts and feelings.

Let others learn about the tool that you have discovered along your path. Send us a copy of your survival tool for possible inclusion in a future edition. If your idea is used, you will receive a complimentary copy of STRESS SURVIVAL KIT Volume II.

Send your ideas to:

STRESS SURVIVAL KIT Vol. II
2501 SE Madison
Portland, OR 97214

Thanks.

Bob and Maggie

Resources

Stress Survival Skills

The authors are avialable for workshops and conference presentations on stress survival. For more information see HEALTHWORKS PRESENTATIONS.

STRESS SURVIVAL KIT

The Kit is a great gift for a friend or coworker in distress.

For more information on bulk orders and site licences for worksites, hospitals, schools and instructors contact, Bob Czimbal.

HEALTHWORKS   2501 SE Madison   Portland, OR   97214   *(503) 232-3522*

Bibliography

Additional Books on Stress and Survival:

Kicking Your Stress Habits.   Donald A Tubesing. Duluth, MN: Whole Person Associates, 1981.

Stress Management for Wellness. Walt Schafer. Orlando, FL: Harcourt Brace Jovanovich, Publishers, 1992.

Transforming Stress into Power. Mark J Tager, M.D. and Stephen Willard. Chicago, IL: Great Performance, Inc., 1988.

The Survivor Personality. Al Siebert. Portland, OR: Practical Psychology Press, 1992

Stress Survival Kit Team

Bob Czimbal   Author

Bob Czimbal's professional background includes Sociology and Community Planning. He founded the Cherry Grove Wellness Center and The Institute for Self-Esteem Enrichment (I. S.E.E.). Currently as Director of HEALTHWORKS, he implements workplace wellness programs and develops motivational tools. A national keynote speaker and trainer, Bob's presentation titles include Enhancing Self-Esteem, The Art of Friendship, Laughing at Life, Teamwork for Success, Yes to Life, Wellness!: A Reverence for Life, Stress Survival Skills and Vitamin T.

Maggie Zadikov   Author

Maggie Zadikov has a Masters degree in Education and has been teaching for twenty years. In 1984, she became a licensed massage therapist. Maggie has worked as a health behavior specialist in smoking cessation and weight management programs. She is an experienced presenter of relaxation skills, massage, eating and weight issues and Vitamin T. Currently, she is studying Oriental Medicine, working toward licensure in acupuncture.

Bob and Maggie have self published: *The F.I.T.ness Game®, Stress Survival Kit* and *A Guide to Healthy Touch: Vitamin T.*

L. Tobin   Editor

With background in both Special Education (M.A.) and Educational Psychology and fifteen years of educational experience in public and private residential settings, Tobin speaks from knowledge and experience. Bilingual in Spanish, with extensive experience in Native American and Alaskan settings, he brings an unusual depth of perspective to his work. His writings also address character development and intuitive problem solving. Trainings are highly practical and skill oriented.

Dodie Setoda   Illustrator

Setoda is a Portland freelance illustrator who enjoys transforming the written word into narrative artwork. She does a variety of commissions working in watercolor, color pencil, pen & ink and graphite.

HEALTHWORKS PRESENTATIONS

by Bob Czimbal

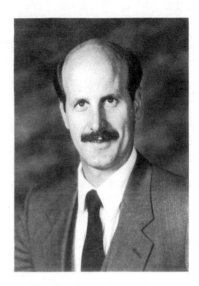

YES to Life!

Laughing at Life

Stress Survival Skills

The Art of Friendship

Enriching Self-Esteem

Teamwork for Success

The F.I.T.ness Game ®

Whistle While You Work

Vitamin T = Healthy Touch

Wellness! A Reverence for Life

Motivation: Awareness to Action

HEALTHWORKS presentations are guaranteed to enliven and enlighten the audience. Bob Czimbal delivers a universal, lighthearted message about health and happiness. They are entertaining, inspiring, and involve a high degree of interaction. Each topic provides the audience with the motivation and skills to convert awareness to action. The goal is to build a sense of community and promote networking. Attendees consistently report they have gained useful skills that will last a lifetime.

HEALTHWORKS presentations are available for conference kickoffs, keynotes, staff development, public seminars, luncheons and evening entertainment. The length of the presentations can vary from one hour to one day. They include handouts, resources, prizes and surprises.

Since 1970, Bob Czimbal has been delivering energetic, uplifting, practical presentations to national corporations, small companies, universities, high schools, day care centers, hospitals, clinics, federal, state and local government agencies.

Bob Czimbal's professional career has included work as a Sociologist, Community Planner, founder of the Cherry Grove Wellness Center, and associate of the Institute for Self-Esteem Enrichment. Bob is author and self-publisher of The F.I.T.ness Game, Vitamin T and Stress Survival Kit. Currently he is director of HEALTHWORKS, a company dedicated to the development and implementation of workplace wellness programs.

For additional information on custom presentations contact HEALTHWORKS to find out how we can be of service to you.

Bob Czimbal   (503) 232-3522
HEALTHWORKS
2501 SE Madison
Portland, OR 97214

YES!

The Lifelong Pursuit of Health & Happiness

By Bob Czimbal

Kick off your conference with a winning keynote...**YES!** Audiences welcome the opportunity to unwind, laugh, move around and make new friends.

YES! means to embrace life. Bob's goal as a motivational speaker is to awaken the inner desire to learn and grow. Bob provides the skills and tools necessary to convert awareness to action.

YES! will build a sense of community and promote networking. Each presentation is customized to complement the theme of the conference.

YES! is the ultimate icebreaker. This learn-by-doing style of presenting is refreshing and energizing. The audience loves to get in on the act. Also included are prizes, surprises and a special guest appearance by "Chief Baba".

"Laughter is aerobic exercise for the spirit."

YES! is a delightful blend of the best of HEALTHWORKS PRESENTATIONS.

Sample list of activities:

Master of Friendship Award
A Cosmic Look at Ourselves
Loosen Up Your Funny Bone
Vitamin T = Healthy Touch
F.I.T.ness Game Contest
The Stress Survival Kit
Self-Esteem Boosters
Good Humor Contest
Teamwork Tricks
The Spirit of Play
Time Well Spent
Common Ground
The Human Knot
Ya Hi ... Ya Huck!
Applause Meter
Team Juggling
Wild and Well
Fun Raisers
Stress Balls
Let's Dance
YES to Life
Moomba
Z Ball

Bob Czimbal (503) 232-3522
HEALTHWORKS
2501 SE Madison
Portland, Oregon   97214

The F.I.T.ness Game ®

The F.I.T.ness Game

An exciting action game that educates and motivates employees to make fitness part of their daily lives. The Game makes fitness **fun, social and rewarding.** A great way to kick off or enhance any health or safety program at the worksite!

Everybody Plays . . .

regardless of age or fitness level. Players earn points for time involved in their choice of over 40 activities from aerobics to walking. Employees earn Game points on their own time. The emphasis is on **F**requency, **I**ntensity, and **T**ime spent exercising. Everybody plays at his or her own pace.

. . . Everybody Wins!

Players earn prizes, awards, recognition and improved fitness. A healthy spirit of competition is encouraged.

WORKSITE APPEAL

Employees enjoy the Game, as shown by consistently high levels of participation over time. The Game can also be shared with family members.

Coordinators find it easy to implement. The program is highly successful in motivating beginners to start a regular exercise program.

Employers benefit from having healthier, happier, more productive workers. The F.I.T.ness Game is a cooperative effort: the company provides the program; the employees provide the sweat.

Years of field testing and independent research have demonstrated that the Game:

- Motivates employees to exercise regularly
- Reduces health care costs
- Reduces body fat levels
- Builds self-esteem
- Is cost-effective

F.I.T.ness Game Starter:

- 10 Player Kits (shown below)
- 5 Team Score Cards
- 100-page Training Manual with masters and artwork
- 10 Incentive Prizes — pencil, pen, luggage tag, mug, Low Fat Grocery List, Fit Foods magnet, Things To Do pad, water bottle, T-shirt, and award medal
- Display Kit — maps, posters, markers

Price: $250

F.I.T.ness Game Sampler:

Player Kit plus Fit Check form, Low Fat Grocery List, Fit Foods magnet, and Things To Do pad.

Price: $25

PLAYER KIT

The **Player Manual** is an individual workbook given to each employee. It contains concise information about the principles of fitness, how to earn points, and ways to make fitness a lifelong adventure.

The **Weekly Score Card** — A pad of individual score cards is provided to encourage regular participation. Score Cards are turned in weekly to be used with the Incentive Program.

The **Team Score Card** is a visual reminder for players to encourage each other to exercise.

Award Certificates are presented to all players as symbols of their achievement.

The F.I.T.ness Game
Everybody Plays . . . Everybody Wins!

The F.I.T.ness Game
Everybody Plays . . . Everybody Wins!

Name (print)

Score Card — Points

Monday
Tuesday
Wednesday
Thursday
Friday
Saturday
Sunday

Total

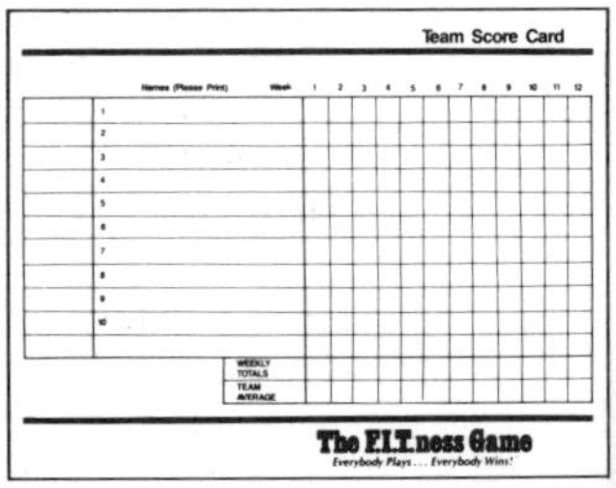

Team Score Card

The F.I.T.ness Game
Everybody Plays . . . Everybody Wins!

The F.I.T.ness Game
Everybody Plays . . . Everybody Wins!

AWARD

This award recognizes the effort and achievement of the above-named player who has earned _____ points in the process of making fitness a lifelong adventure.

Conferred in recognition this

_____ day of _____, 19 _____

Signed _____

TiME WELL SPENT

A unique **52-week appointment planner** that includes time management suggestions, high performance tips and stress management information.

Time Well Spent is like purchasing *three books in one:*

Time Management
An undated planner you can begin right away — with all the features you've come to expect:

- weekly appointment pages
- to-do lists
- weekly goals
- expense records
- telephone numbers, etc.

Performance Tips
Each week you'll learn energizing tips for body and mind that will increase your performance and effectiveness throughout your day.

- stress relaxers
- energizing activities
- inspiring quotes
- affirmations
- nutrition tips

Stress Management
Time Well Spent contains concise, practical stress management information. Each week, new suggestions. The perfect introduction for those too busy (or stressed out) to read a whole book!

All this is available to you in one convenient planner.

Get Organized, Get Energized
Time Well Spent is all you need to create the time and energy for the most productive year of your life.

Take care of business while you take care of yourself. That's Time Well Spent.

WORKSITE APPEAL

Offer your employees a healthy alternative to the traditional office planner. Dated and customized company editions are available.

Time Well Spent is the perfect incentive gift for any wellness program.

Price: $15

> *Happiness is not a state to arrive at, but a manner of traveling.* MARGARET LEE RUNBECK

	Priorities This Week			To Do
This month's Mondays	Complete	Start	To Pay	

Mon — Lunch / Planned Break / Evening

Tue — Lunch / Planned Break / Evening

Wed — Lunch / Planned Break / Evening — Pleasant Thoughts

Thu — Lunch / Planned Break / Evening

Fri — Lunch / Planned Break / Evening

Nutrition Tip #1
OFFICE BEVERAGES. Stock office with nutritious drinks. Fruit juices diluted 50% with sparkling water make refreshing boosts in place of soda or coffee. Stock variety. Celery and pineapple for summer drinks. Try fresh carrot juice for a boost to immune system and for eye care; black cherry for iron and oxygen intake, or vegetable juice/broth of carrots/potato/beets/celery. Recipe books are available. Serve in stemware to visitors for that "class" act.

Sat

Sun

Well-Rounded Weekend:
☐ Friends/Family
☐ Active/Adventure
☐ Quiet/Spiritual
☐ Creative/Crafts

Time Management — Suggestions
Mark two ideas you will use this week.
☐ Consolidate similar tasks ☐ Increase planning time
☐ Complete by priority ☐ Keep work area organized
☐ Handle paper only once ☐ Complete tasks on time
☐ Arrange uninterrupted times ☐ Alter pace of activities
☐ Finish each task before moving on ☐ Break down large projects into parts

Notes

Time Well Spent™

I actively create the positive qualities of my day.

41

TiME WELL SPENT
A
STRESS REDUCTION
APPOINTMENT PLANNER
FOR
BUSINESS AND HEALTH
LARRY TOBIN, M.Ed.

Put The F.I.T.ness Game and Time Well Spent to work for you.

Vitamin T is the "nurturing nutrient" found in healthy **TOUCH.** The US Department of Health and Happiness has established that Vitamin T is essential for every body. Daily doses promote growth.

Natural sources of Vitamin T are handshakes, hugs, kisses, cuddles and rubs obtained from family and friends. Vitamin T is absorbed through the skin and helps to soothe the body, calm the mind, warm the heart and nourish the spirit.

Vitamin T restores sense of humor and strengthens self-esteem. Positively habit-forming. Guaranteed safe for all ages. Give with permission only. Keep within reach of children. Active ingredient: TLC.

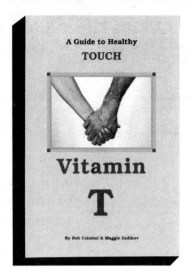

A Guide to Healthy
TOUCH

Vitamin T

By Bob Czimbal & Maggie Zadikov

Vitamin T   A Guide to Healthy Touch
by Bob Czimbal and Maggie Zadikov
Softcover, 200 pages,7x10
30 illustrations   ISBN 1-878793-00-4
Price $14.00

The Vitamin T book contains:

• Examples of over 100 fun ways to exchange Vitamin T
• Guidelines for healthy touch at home, school and work
• Skills to cure Vitamin T deficiencies, like loneliness
• Techniques for the prevention of sexual harassment and abuse
• Ways to enhance intimacy and healthy sexuality
• Systems for creating an abundance of Vitamin T
• Tools to heal painful touches called ouches (Touch minus T = ouch).

Vitamin T
®
I AM A HEALTHY SOURCE

Vitamin T Jar Includes:
• Instruction label
• 24 prescription cards
  "Good For One Dose of Vitamin T"
• Lapel Pin: 1" diameter 4-color enamel pin
* Extra lapel pins available @ $4 each.
Price $10.00

Workshops: Healthy Touch at Work
by HEALTHWORKS SEMINARS

HEALTHWORKS 2501 SE Madison Portland, OR 97214 (503) 232-3522